Polar Lands

Joy Palmer

Watts Books
London • New York • Sydney

© Watts Books 1991
Paperback edition 1995

Watts Books
96 Leonard Street
London EC2A 4RH

Franklin Watts Australia
14 Mars Road
Lane Cove
NSW 2066

ISBN: 0 7496 0574 X (hardback)
ISBN: 0 7496 2318 7 (paperback)

10 9 8 7 6 5 4 3 2 1

Editor: A. Patricia Sechi
Designer: Shaun Barlow
Cover Design: K and Co
Artwork: David Farren
Cover Artwork: Hayward Art Group

Educational Advisor: Joy Richardson
Consultant: Miranda MacQuitty

A CIP catalogue record for this book
is available from the British Library

Printed in Italy
by G. Canale & Co. SpA

Contents

What are polar lands?

The polar lands are the coldest places in the world. For much of the year the polar lands are frozen. Most of the land is covered in snow or ice. Few animals live here all year round. The winters are dark with hardly any daylight. In summer it is warmer and much brighter.

▽ The thick ice stretches as far as you can see.

Where are polar lands?

The polar lands lie near the North Pole and the South Pole, at the ends of the earth. The **Arctic** is the most northern part of the world. It is mainly frozen ocean. The **Antarctic** is the area around the South Pole. Antarctica is the land around the South Pole, surrounded by cold seas.

▷ There is no land under the North Pole, only ice.

▽ The polar lands lie at the top and bottom of the earth.

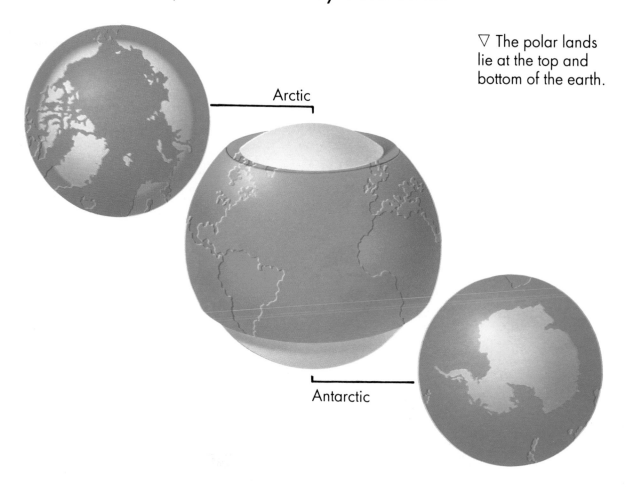

Arctic

Antarctic

What are polar lands like?

Both the Arctic and the Antarctic are almost completely covered in ice or snow for most of the year. During the summer the snow and ice begin to melt. People have learnt to live on the icy land around the Arctic. Recently people have gone to live at the Antarctic too.

▷ In summer the snow begins to melt in the Antarctic and the land shows beneath the ice.

▽ People in the Arctic have learnt how to survive in harsh weather.

Why is it cold?

The North and South Poles are cold because of the way the earth moves around the sun. The sun's rays are not very strong at the poles. In winter, the weather becomes even colder and more of the oceans freeze. Strong winds drive snow over the land in storms called **blizzards**.

▷ In mid-summer the sky is bright all day and night in the Arctic.

▽ As winter arrives, the sun never rises very high in the sky. The sun sets only a few hours after rising in the sky.

Plants

Few plants are able to grow in polar lands because of the cold. The seeds of some plants are very strong. They may live for years under the snow, then burst into life during a warm enough summer. Tough grass and plants such as **moss** and **lichen** grow in the Arctic. Many lie close to the ground to survive the cold.

▽ The Arctic willow plant is a tiny tree.

▽ The Arctic buttercup grows and flowers during the summer.

▷ Tussock grass grows on many islands in the Antarctic.

▽ Lichens cling to rocks in the Antarctic.

▷ Mosses are one of the most common plants growing in the Arctic.

▷ The saxifrage plant has purple flowers and lies very close to the ground.

▽ Brightly coloured plants burst into life during the short Arctic summer.

Animals of the Arctic

Animals live in the Arctic all year round, but some only come when the weather is warmer. Most polar animals have short legs and thick fur to help them survive the cold. Seals have a thick layer of fat, called **blubber**, to protect them from the cold.

▷ Musk oxen in the Arctic have long, thick hair to keep them warm.

▽ The Arctic fox sheds its brown coat in winter and grows a white coat.

△ Walruses have long white tusks and thick crinkly skin.

◁ The ringed seal is just one of the many kinds of seal living in the Arctic.

◁ Caribou have large feet which help them to move across the ice.

▽ Polar bears spend their lives on the Arctic ice.

13

Animals of the Antarctic

The oceans around Antarctica are home to many different animals, but few animals spend all year on the ice covering Antarctica. Whales make their home there during the summer. Many kinds of seals and birds live on the edge of the ice. They dive into the sea in search of food.

▽ Giant orange sea spiders live on the sea floor.

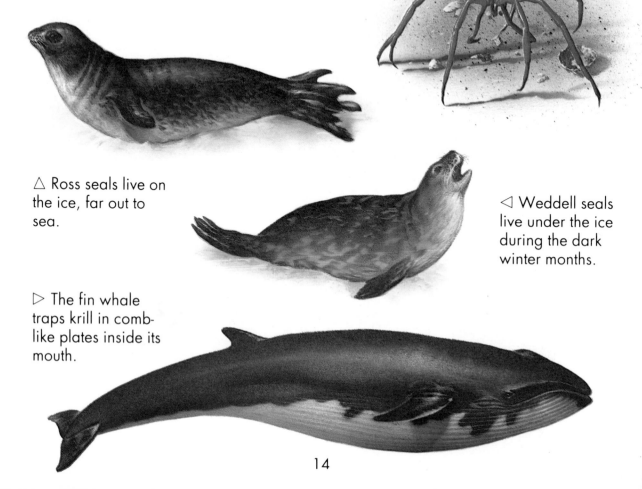

△ Ross seals live on the ice, far out to sea.

◁ Weddell seals live under the ice during the dark winter months.

▷ The fin whale traps krill in comb-like plates inside its mouth.

△ The blue whale is
the largest animal
on earth.

▷ Leopard seals
hunt other seals and
eat penguins.

▽ Krill are tiny sea creatures which look like shrimps.

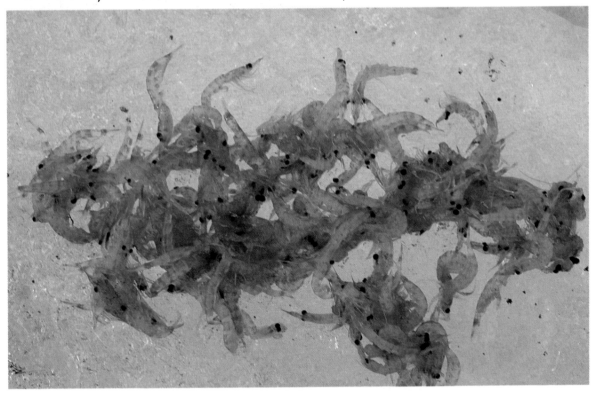

Birds

Penguins live at the Antarctic and not at the Arctic. Close to the shore, young penguins hatch from their eggs. The parents fetch food for them to eat. Few birds live at the Arctic all year round. Most birds only live in the polar lands for the summer and fly somewhere warmer for the winter.

▽ The emperor penguin is the largest bird in the penguin family.

▽ The king penguin lives on islands near the Antarctic.

▽ The little auk is a seabird which lives at the Arctic.

▽ The Arctic tern flies from one Pole to another to catch the summer.

▷ The ptarmigan has brown feathers in summer and white feathers in winter.

◁ The adelie penguin is the most common penguin found in the Antarctic.

◁ The snowy owl keeps its almost white feathers all year round. It feeds on animals.

People

In the Arctic people have learnt to live in the cold. The Inuit, the Yakut and the Lapps are three peoples of the Arctic. Some polar people still follow old ways of life. They hunt or keep herds of animals. But many have settled in towns and live in modern homes. People only visit Antarctica. They do not settle there.

▷ These Inuit children learn to fish and hunt in the school holidays.

▽ The Yakut live in north Asia. They breed dogs and reindeer.

▽ The Inuit people live in North America, the Soviet Union and Greenland.

△ The Lapp people live in northern Europe.

How the people live

In winter, people in the Arctic do not catch the bus to town. They go on a snowmobile. These are like motor scooters on skis which cross the ice more easily than using wheels. To keep warm, people at the poles wear padded clothes. Animal skins used to be stitched together to make clothes.

▷ Scientists and explorers visiting the Antarctic stay at research stations.

▽ People at the Arctic live in modern houses and travel on snowmobiles.

Surviving in the polar lands

People and animals of the poles have learnt to survive these harsh lands. Penguins cluster together because there is little land. Polar bears keep their babies in a burrow beneath the ice to keep them safe. In the past Arctic people only ate meat and fish. It is too cold to grow fruit and vegetables.

▷ Arctic people wear many layers of clothes. Some clothes are still made of skins.

▽ Polar bears keep their babies in a burrow below the ice until the winter has passed.

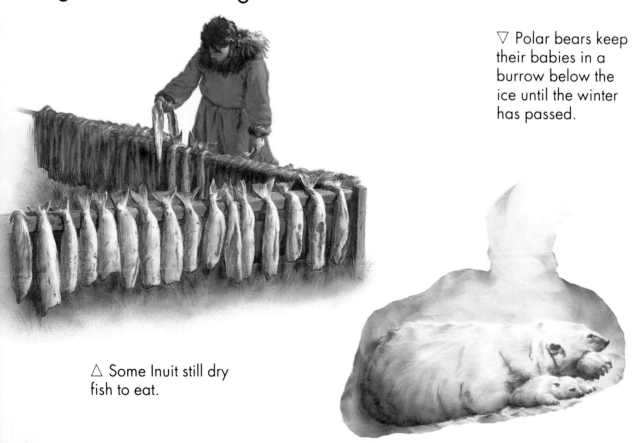

△ Some Inuit still dry fish to eat.

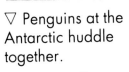

▽ Penguins at the Antarctic huddle together.

△ Some Arctic people hunt seals for their skins.

Importance of the poles

Polar lands are important places on our planet. Scientists learn about the world's weather by studying the ice and temperature at the poles. The Antarctic is one of the world's last wild places. We must save the animals which live there. They are different from others in the world.

▷ Scientists carry out weather tests at the poles.

▽ The Antarctic is one of the last unspoilt places on earth.

Threats to the poles

The Arctic is **mined** for coal, metals and oil. As more people settle and work in the polar lands, animals and plants may be harmed. Too much fishing and hunting also endanger the animals.

The earth is becoming warmer. If polar ice melts, the level of the oceans will rise and flood the land.

▷ Oil is mined in some of the countries around the Arctic.

▽ Whales are protected animals, but they are still hunted by some countries.

▽ Polar bears look
for food amongst
rubbish near Arctic
settlements.

Protecting the poles

We can help to protect the polar lands by using fewer aerosol sprays. These destroy a part of the **atmosphere**, called the ozone layer. It protects the earth from the sun's heat. We need to burn fewer **fuels**. These cause heat to be trapped in the air making the air around the earth warm up.

▷ Groups such as Greenpeace fight to keep the poles clean and unspoilt.

▽ Many sprays are now worked by using a pump and not aerosols to spread the liquid inside.

Things to do

- Make a poster to try to persuade people not to use aerosol sprays. Hang it up at school or in your window at home.

- Grow some cress seeds in two saucers to see why plants do not grow easily in the polar lands. Put one saucer in the fridge and the other one in a warm place. After a few days look at the results.

Useful addresses:

Friends of the Earth
26-28 Underwood Street
London N1 7JQ

Greenpeace Ltd.
30 Islington Green
London N1

Glossary

Antarctic The area around the South Pole. It includes the large area of land called Antarctica.

Arctic The large cold area around the North Pole.

atmosphere The layer of gases which surround the earth.

blizzard A snow storm when the wind blows the snow across the land.

blubber The thick layer of fat which seals, whales and penguins have. It helps protect them against the cold.

caribou An animal with hoofs and antlers. It is part of the reindeer family.

fuel A substance which burns and gives energy. Coal and oil are fuels.

lichen A plant which does not flower. It grows close to the ground and on rocks.

mineral A mineral is any substance, which is not alive, which can be dug out of the ground. Coal, gold and diamonds are minerals.

mining Digging minerals out of the ground.

moss A simple plant which grows near the ground in closely packed clusters.

research station Settlements where scientists come and stay to study and to do research.

31

Index

Photographic credits: B & C
Alexander 23, (M Jacques) 7,
(P Drummond) 21; Bruce Coleman
(S J Krasemann) 5, (Dr E Pott) 9,
(H Reinhard) 13, (B & C
Alexander) 19, Greenpeace
(Culley) 15, 25, (Morgan) 29;
NHPA (J Chester) 3, (J Shaw) 11;
Zefa (H Groendal) 27.